T0389827

TOP 10

ANIMAL EXTREMES

THE 10 COOLEST ANIMALS

BY RACHEL ROSE

BEARPORT
PUBLISHING

Minneapolis, Minnesota

Credits

Cover and title page, © Design Pics Inc/Alamy Stock Photo, © mariusz_prusaczyk/iStock, and © Kufner-Foto/iStock; Title Page, © Design Pics Inc/Alamy Stock Photo; 4, © Yü Lan/Adobe Stock Photos; 5, © Christian Hütter/Alamy Stock Photo, © Diego Grandi/Shutterstock; 6–7, © Todd Mintz/Alamy Stock Photo, © Doc White/ Blue Planet Archive; 8, © Stan Tekiela Author / Naturalist / Wildlife Photographer/Getty Images; 9, © Sourabh/Adobe Stock Photos; 10, © MarcoDiaz/Adobe Stock Photos; 10–11, © Lukas Kovarik/Alamy Stock Photo; 12, © Winfried Wisniewski/Getty Images; 12–13, © StuPorts/iStock; 14, © Thorsten Spoerlein/iStock; 15, © VPC Animals Photo/Alamy Stock Photo; 16–17, © Asim Patel/iStock; 17, © andyschar/iStock; 18–19, © owngarden/Getty Images; 20, © USO/iStock; 20–21, © guenterguni/Getty Images; 22T, © Dodge65/iStock; 22M, © mofles/ iStock; 22B, © Nature Picture Library/Alamy Stock Photo; 23, © Bryngelzon/iStock.

Bearport Publishing Company Product Development Team

Publisher: Jen Jenson; Director of Product Development: Spencer Brinker; Managing Editor: Allison Juda; Editor: Cole Nelson; Associate Editor: Naomi Reich; Associate Editor: Tiana Tran; Art Director: Colin O'Dea; Designer: Kim Jones; Designer: Kayla Eggert; Product Development Specialist: Owen Hamlin

Statement on Usage of Generative Artificial Intelligence

Bearport Publishing remains committed to publishing high-quality nonfiction books. Therefore, we restrict the use of generative AI to ensure accuracy of all text and visual components pertaining to a book's subject. See BearportPublishing.com for details.

Library of Congress Cataloging-in-Publication Data is available at www.loc.gov or upon request from the publisher.

ISBN: 979-8-89232-637-7 (hardcover)
ISBN: 979-8-89232-686-5 (ebook)

For more information, write to Bearport Publishing, 5357 Penn Avenue South, Minneapolis, MN 55419.

CONTENTS

PLAYING IT COOL

Earth is home to millions of **species** of animals. They come in all shapes, colors, and sizes. Some are strong, some are smart, and some are deadly. But there are also a lot of animals that are supercool.

WHAT ARE THE WILD WORLD'S 10 COOLEST CREATURES?

Read on to decide for yourself. . . .

#10 GIANT ANTEATER

Slurp! A giant anteater flicks out its long tongue to catch tiny prey. The 2-foot (0.6-m) tongue is covered in sticky saliva to trap ants and **termites** for a tasty feast. In addition to being long, this special tongue is superfast. The anteater can flick it up to 150 times per minute. Now, that's speedy!

They can eat up to 30,000 ants and termites a day.

Anteaters walk with their claws off the ground. This keeps them sharp for digging.

Anteaters have no teeth.

#9 NARWHAL

Nobody has ever seen a unicorn. But people have spotted the unicorn of the sea! Narwhals are ocean **mammals** with hornlike tusks growing out of their heads. Scientists believe narwhals use their tusks to **communicate** with one another, hunt prey, fight predators, and attract **mates**.

Narwhals change color from gray to white as they grow older.

Most male narwhals have tusks, but only some females grow them.

These sea unicorns can live for up to 50 years.

The tusk is an extralong tooth that can grow up to 10 ft. (3 m) long.

#8 STAR-NOSED MOLE

Twinkle, twinkle, little star . . . nose? The star-nosed mole has 22 fleshy **tentacles** around its **nostrils** that form a starlike shape. Because it has poor vision, this mole uses its wiggly tentacles to make its way. The tentacles help this furry creature feel through underground tunnels where it lives. In fact, its snout tentacles can touch up to 12 things each second!

Star-nosed moles can swim and smell underwater.

They are often found near forests, lakes, and marshes.

This mole can eat a worm in a fraction of a second.

#7 PEACOCK

It's showtime! A peacock is a male peafowl bird with a striking blue-and-green tail. This bird uses its beautiful tail to attract a mate. First, the peacock spreads its tail feathers wide like a fan. Then, it struts back and forth while shaking its booty in a special dance. A female, called a peahen, chooses the male with the longest, most colorful tail and best dance moves.

Peacock tails usually start growing when the birds are two or three years old.

Each shake in a mating dance makes a rattling noise.

These birds also make a honking sound when looking for a mate.

#6 SLOTH

Look up! Sloths spend most of their time hanging upside down high up in trees. They can even sleep that way! When sloths do move, it's very slowly. They travel only about 41 yards (37 m) per day. That's less than half the length of a football field! These slowpokes come down from their trees about once a week to pee and poop. Then, they slowly climb their way back up!

Sloths use their claws to drag themselves along the ground.

A sloth's claws can be up to 4 inches (10 cm) long.

Sloths swim! They move three times faster in water than on land.

Because of the coloring of their mouth fur, some sloths look like they're always smiling.

It can sometimes take a sloth a whole day to climb a tree.

#5 CHEETAH

Want to race—and lose? Cheetahs can run up to 70 miles per hour (110 kph). Meanwhile, the fastest a human has ever run is only 27 mph (43 kph). These big cats are the fastest land mammals on Earth. *Zoom!* They use their lightning speed to hunt prey. Cheetahs can go from 0 to 60 mph (97 kph) in just 3 seconds!

From big antelopes to small hares, cheetahs can take down almost any animal.

Cheetahs don't roar like a lion. Instead, they meow like a cat.

They have excellent eyesight, spotting their prey from up to 1 mile (2 km) away.

A **flexible** spine helps these spotted animals run fast.

Cheetahs have more than 1,000 spots on their fur!

13

#4 OKAPI

Is that a zebr-affe? An okapi's top half looks a lot like its giraffe cousin. Meanwhile, its butt and legs are striped like a zebra. A giraffe-like long neck and tongue helps the animal eat leaves high in the forest. The striped behind allows it to hide in the shadows of trees. This keeps the okapi safe from predators.

An okapi's tongue can grow up to 14 in. (36 cm) long.

Okapis can lick their own ears!

Rotating ears help okapis listen for sounds in all directions.

The zebra-like pattern helps a baby okapi spot its mother even in the dark forest.

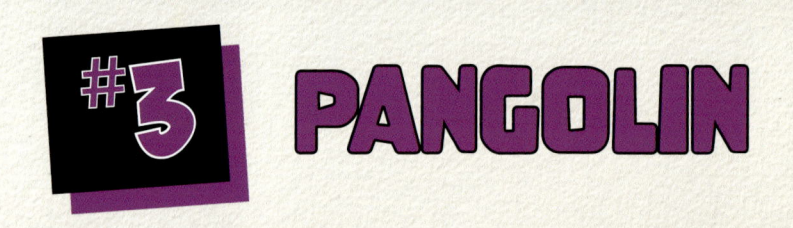

#3 PANGOLIN

Check out that armor! Pangolins are covered in hard scales. When under attack from hungry predators, they roll themselves up into a tight ball. Pangolin scales are so strong that not even a lion can bite through them. Each scale is made of **keratin**—the same **protein** found in human nails.

When eating, they close their ears and nostrils to keep insects out.

Pangolins also have powerful tails for protection.

A pangolin can squirt a stinky liquid from its tail to keep predators away.

Pangolins are the only mammals covered in scales.

#2 MANDRILL

Meet the biggest, brightest monkeys on Earth. Male mandrills are large and colorful. Their brilliant color is a sign of their strength. The more colorful male mandrills are, the more success they have in finding a mate. Purple-colored rumps also help groups of mandrills stick together as they move through their forest homes. It's hard to miss those bright butts!

Male mandrills can weigh up to 77 pounds (35 kg). Females weigh about half as much.

Mandrills live in large groups called hordes.

These big monkeys scream, grunt, growl, and bark to communicate.

Pouches inside their mouths and necks can store food.

#1 KOMODO DRAGON

Although dragons aren't real, Komodo dragons are! They are the world's largest lizards. Males can grow up to 10 ft. (3 m) long. Komodo dragons hunt by chomping down on their prey with a **venomous** bite. *Munch!* Days later, the bitten animals die from the poison. Then, the dragons use their powerful sense of smell to find the bodies, and dinner is served!

Young Komodo dragons can climb trees to escape danger.

These powerful lizards have been roaming Earth for about four million years.

They can run up to 13 mph (21 kph).

Komodo dragons weigh in at around 300 lbs. (136 kg).

Komodo dragons smell the air by flicking their long tongues.

EVEN MORE
COOL ANIMALS

These 10 animals aren't the only cool ones in the wild. What are some other awesome creatures?

ARCTIC TERN

These extraordinary birds can travel about 1.8 million miles (3 million km) over a lifetime. That's more than three trips to the moon and back!

JAPANESE SPIDER CRAB

Japanese spider crabs are the world's largest crabs. They can measure a whopping 12.5 ft. (3.8 m) across.

FLYING SQUIRREL

These bushy-tailed animals glide from tree to tree, using a special flap of skin between their front and back legs.

GLOSSARY

communicate to pass information between two or more things

flexible able to bend easily

keratin a protein found in nails and hair

mammals warm-blooded animals that have hair and feed babies milk from their bodies

mates partners that come together to have babies

nostrils openings in the nose that are used for breathing and smelling

protein a kind of substance that keeps the body healthy and strong

rotating turning around

species groups that animals are divided into, according to similar characteristics

tentacles long, hanging body parts that come out of an animal's body

termites insects that eat wood

venomous full of poison that is released through a sting or bite

INDEX

READ MORE

Bradley, Doug. *Animal Behavior (Discover More: The Lives of Animals).* Buffalo, NY: Britannica Educational Publishing, 2024.

Johnson, Robin. *Animal Celebrities (Astonishing Animals).* New York: Crabtree Publishing Company, 2020.

LEARN MORE ONLINE

1. Go to **FactSurfer.com** or scan the QR code below.

2. Enter "**10 Coolest Animals**" into the search box.

3. Click on the cover of this book to see a list of websites.

ABOUT THE AUTHOR

Rachel Rose writes books for kids and teaches yoga. Her favorite animal for all time is her dog, Sandy.